The Awesome Autistic Guide
to Feelings and Emotions

Part of the *Awesome Autistic Guides* series

The *Awesome Autistic Guides* series explores many experiences you might have as an autistic young person. The authors are autistic adults who understand a bit of what it's like to be you, and have some idea of what might lie ahead. They'll help you discover your own strengths, manage your challenges, boost your confidence, and figure out ways to enjoy being autistic, like they do.

Also part of the Awesome Autistic Guides *series*

The Awesome Autistic Guide to Other Humans
Relationships with Friends and Family
Yenn Purkis and Tanya Masterman
Illustrated by Glynn Masterman
ISBN 978 1 83997 740 4
eISBN 978 1 83997 741 1

The Awesome Autistic Guide to Being Proud
Feeling Good About Who You Are
Yenn Purkis and Tanya Masterman
Illustrated by Glynn Masterman
ISBN 978 1 83997 736 7
eISBN 978 1 83997 737 4

The Awesome Autistic Go-To Guide
A Practical Handbook for Autistic Teens and Tweens
Yenn Purkis and Tanya Masterman
Foreword by Emma Goodall
Illustrated by Glynn Masterman
ISBN 978 1 78775 316 7
eISBN 978 1 78775 317 4

By the same authors

The Awesome Autistic Guide for Trans Teens
Yenn Purkis and Sam Rose
Illustrated by Glynn Masterman
ISBN 978 1 83997 076 4
eISBN 978 1 83997 077 1

The Autism and Neurodiversity Self Advocacy Handbook
Developing the Skills to Determine Your Own Future
Yenn Purkis and Barb Cook
ISBN 978 1 78775 575 8
eISBN 978 1 78775 576 5

THE AWESOME AUTISTIC GUIDE TO FEELINGS AND EMOTIONS

Finding Your Comfort Zone

Yenn Purkis and **Tanya Masterman**

Illustrated by Glynn Masterman

Jessica Kingsley Publishers
London and Philadelphia

First published in Great Britain in 2024 by Jessica Kingsley Publishers
An imprint of John Murray Press

1

A CIP catalogue record for this title is available from
the British Library and the Library of Congress

ISBN 978 1 83997 738 1
eISBN 978 1 83997 739 8

Printed and bound in Great Britain by Clays Ltd

Jessica Kingsley Publishers' policy is to use papers that are natural,
renewable and recyclable products and made from wood grown in
sustainable forests. The logging and manufacturing processes are expected
to conform to the environmental regulations of the country of origin.

Jessica Kingsley Publishers
Carmelite House
50 Victoria Embankment
London EC4Y 0DZ

www.jkp.com

John Murray Press
Part of Hodder & Stoughton Ltd
An Hachette Company

Contents

Introduction

Hi there! Welcome to this book. This book is all about feelings and emotions for autistic kids, like you. This might be a topic that you find difficult or boring, or can't see the point of, but it's very important. This book will help you to understand your own feelings and find out what to do if they get too big and scary.

The two authors of this book, Tanya and Yenn, are also autistic. Many years ago, we were kids – just like you. Well, not exactly like you, because everyone's a bit different. We can use our experience to try and help autistic young people to understand things like their feelings and emotions.

ABOUT YENN

Yenn is an autistic author. Yenn also has attention deficit hyperactivity disorder (ADHD) and schizophrenia and is non-binary gender. Yenn gives talks about autism all over the world and also works as a government official in Australia. Yenn loves cats and is also an artist. Yenn's favourite thing in the world is writing books. Yenn has an older brother and a mum and dad.

ABOUT TANYA

Tanya is also an autistic ADHDer, but she didn't find out until she had a child (now a teen) who is also an AuDHDer (this word is a mashup of autism and ADHD). Like Yenn, Tanya works for the government in Australia and loves cats (she has one called Moki), but she makes things with yarn instead of making pictures and poetry. Tanya's husband, Glynn, has ADHD and did the illustrations in this book.

ABOUT MIN

Before we get started, we need to introduce you to Min. You will see Min in every chapter of this book. Min is a meerkat, and they are autistic. We don't actually know if you can get autistic meerkats, but we thought it would be fun to have pictures of meerkats instead of people. Min lives with their family, and there are lots of other meerkat families nearby, as well as other animals. Min goes to school and their favourite subjects are art, design and anything to do with making things (except cooking, because it sometimes smells bad). We can talk about Min's feelings and how they make their brain feel comfortable. You can tell Min apart from the other meerkats because their eye patches look like glasses, or an infinity symbol. Sometimes Min likes to wear headphones too.

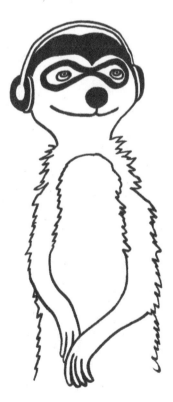

This book will help you to understand what emotions you might be feeling, what your 'comfort zone' is and ways to stay calm. There are lots of activities and fun illustrations too. We hope you enjoy the book and that it helps you understand your feelings and find your own emotional comfort zone.

⇒ Chapter 1 ⇐

What Is the Comfort Zone?

This book is all about how to help your brain and the rest of your body feel comfortable. Sometimes, if our brain doesn't feel okay, the rest of our body doesn't feel okay either. The opposite can happen too. That's true for all people, but it can often be a bit tricky for autistic people, because there are lots of things in the world that make us feel **not** comfortable, and sometimes it can be hard to know how our bodies feel.

FEELING COMFORTABLE

So, what do we mean when we say our brains and bodies feel comfortable? 'Comfort' is a bit of an odd word – it might make you think of a squishy bean bag, or a hammock. But we can't put just our brains in a bean bag or a hammock!

You could also use words like:

- calm

- chilled out

- relaxed

- content

- restful

- serene.

What things do those words make you think about? Maybe a cat sleeping on a bed in a patch of sunlight? Or a still, clear lake with hardly any ripples? Or maybe focusing hard on something that you enjoy? Maybe nothing? We will talk a bit more about this later in the book.

You've probably heard people talk about 'emotions'. In this book, we will talk about what they are, where they come from and some ways to deal with **big** emotions, to help us get back into our comfort zone.

FEELINGS AND EMOTIONS

What IS an emotion? It's our brain's response to something that's happening (or has happened, or could or will happen). It could be from something inside our body, or outside our body. It could be because of something that isn't even real, like being afraid that you might get teleported to Saturn if you walk into your wardrobe on Tuesday morning.

It could be because another person did something or said something that you like or don't like. It could be because of sensory overload, like when there is too much light or noise. If something in your body hurts, you might feel sad, or annoyed. If something great is going to happen tomorrow, like getting a new graphic novel in your favourite series, you might feel excited.

But being able to make a list of emotions doesn't mean we know how they feel. Sometimes an emotion makes us feel things in our body and sometimes not. Have you ever felt that ticklish or squirmy feeling inside your tummy? You might even have felt a bit sick in your tummy, as if you need to throw up, even if you weren't actually ill. Sometimes people say, 'I have butterflies in my tummy' but that's just silly because butterflies couldn't live in there. But it can feel a bit like something is fluttering around. It's what we might feel if we are a bit scared or worried or even excited. We will find out in Chapter 2 why that happens. Hint – it's got nothing to do with butterflies or other insects!

MIN'S ECOLOGY PRESENTATION

We've already met Min. Min is only six months old but that's like a person being about ten years old because meerkats don't live as long as humans do, and they grow up much more quickly. Min likes some of the things at school, like the lunchtime ecology club. But that comes with some not-so-good stuff too – the members of the club have to do a presentation in assembly. Min has been feeling sick in their tummy worrying about it. When they think about talking in front of the school, they are so worried they cannot think of any words to use and know they will not be able to speak. Min tells their teacher about how they are feeling and they decide together that Min can be in charge of making a slide show for the presentation, instead of talking. Min uses some great progress photos of their seedlings and the worm farm. Min stops feeling sick in their tummy because they don't have to talk. Maybe one day Min will feel comfortable doing a talk for their class and maybe they won't – either way is fine.

WHY DO EMOTIONS MATTER?

Emotions are important because they can give us clues about what our bodies and brains need to feel comfortable. They are like messages to ourselves – that's kind of cool, isn't it? So, it's a good idea to spend some time thinking about them, even though it's a bit tricky and not that interesting. Nowhere near as interesting as your favourite game, for example, that's for sure! But it can help us to feel happier and calmer and most of us like those feelings more than feeling angry or sad.

Sometimes our emotions can lead to actions that hurt us, or other people. That's true for everyone. Emotions can tell us that we need to do something to help our brains and bodies feel comfortable. If we pay attention to our brains and bodies, and do those things, it's easier to get into our comfort zone.

IS THE COMFORT ZONE ONLY ABOUT BEING HAPPY?

What do you think we mean when we talk about the emotional comfort zone? Does it mean that a person doesn't have any emotions? Do you think it means that you are happy all the time? That isn't the way emotions work for most people. For most of us, emotions are a bit like a rollercoaster. They might be 'up' (happy or excited) one day and 'down' (sad or frustrated) the next day. Emotions can change quickly. And for autistic people (like us) – and autistic meerkats like Min! – emotions can be scary and confusing as often we can't pinpoint which emotion is happening and why.

What does your comfort zone feel like? What are you doing when you are in your comfort zone? Tanya would be knitting and listening to an audio book or watching a show using noise-cancelling headphones. Or she might be building something from Lego – Star Wars Lego is her favourite. Yenn would be writing a book or a blog post, listening to music or talking to an audience about autism.

If Min was in their comfort zone, they would be making some art or building something, probably listening to music on headphones while they did it.

ACTIVITY: Your comfort zone

List, below or on a piece of paper, three things/ activities that help you to be in your comfort zone.

. . . .

. . . .

. . . .

The 'comfort zone' doesn't mean having no emotions or only being happy. The comfort zone means having emotions that are regulated. What does that mean? 'Regulated' is a big word that means emotions are in balance and not causing stress and confusion. Even emotions like feeling sad can be part of the comfort zone.

In the next few chapters, we will look at feelings, emotions and sensations and how to get into your comfort zone.

⇒ Chapter 2 ⇐

Where Do Emotions Come From?

ARE MY EMOTIONS NORMAL?

In this chapter, we will find out that emotions come from our brains, and then sometimes things happen in our bodies because of our emotions. Everyone's brain is different, but there are some common ways that people experience an emotion. One example is feeling sad. Lots of people cry if they are sad. But some people might not cry; they might just sit quietly and not want to communicate with anybody. Some people might feel that they need to do something with their hands. When Tanya's mum died, she didn't cry at all and didn't have any sad feelings in her body, but she didn't feel quite right. So, she collected all her mum's recipes and turned them into a book and that helped her get back into her comfort zone. Some people thought she was weird and horrible because she didn't cry, but that's not okay – people manage their emotions in different ways.

And sometimes other things make people cry as well. Someone might cry if they are very frustrated, or if they are angry, or if they hear a beautiful piece of music. Min gets very frustrated if one of their buildings is not working out how they hoped it would. Have you felt like that? We certainly have! Sometimes Min will cry and sometimes they might push the building over.

There aren't any 'wrong' emotions. If anyone ever tells you that your feelings or emotions are silly or you're overreacting about something, that's not okay. It's great if they try and support you to work through that emotion, but your emotions are **yours** and they are always the **right** ones for you.

ARE EMOTIONS GOOD OR BAD?

People sometimes divide emotions into good and bad, or positive and negative. But, if you've seen that movie, *Inside Out*, you might know that it's important to have 'bad' or 'negative' emotions like sadness, to help us feel balanced. It's normal to have those sorts of emotions. How does that work? Imagine if your friend was moving away but you were used to seeing them every day and you had heaps of fun together. Feeling sad about it would be the usual way to feel. Most people would not feel happy that they weren't going to see their friend any more. In that situation, your emotional comfort zone would be feeling sad.

Emotions are not really 'good' or 'bad'. There is usually at least one situation where a 'bad' emotion is the most common response. Another example is anger. Some people think that anger is a bad emotion, and we should hide it, but, if someone steals your money, then anger is the usual emotion. And if you are being bullied, once again, anger at the bully is a more helpful emotion than blaming yourself. Being angry can give us more energy to do something about the thing that made us feel angry in the first place. It's like Greta Thunberg being angry about climate change and doing something about it.

ACTIVITY: 'Good' and 'bad' emotions

Write down, below or on a piece of paper, three emotions that you can think of. Do you think the emotions are 'good' or 'bad'?

. . . .

. . . .

. . . .

Next to each emotion, write why you think they are good or bad. Can you think of any situation where an emotion you usually think is 'bad' is actually helpful (such as Yenn feeling anger when someone stole their money)?

CHEMICALS IN OUR BODIES

So now we know that emotions are how our brains respond to things, and sometimes emotions cause feelings or sensations in our bodies too. But how? And what feelings or sensations? And what if we don't feel anything? These are all very complicated things that lots of scientists have studied, and there is still **a lot** that we don't know about how our brains work. We probably don't know that much about meerkat brains either!

You might have heard people talk about chemicals as if they're a bad thing: 'I won't have chemicals in my house.' Some chemicals can be very dangerous, like strong acid or an explosive. But not all chemicals are bad — some we need in order to live. Some are one substance alone (like carbon), or one element mixed with another element, like hydrogen and oxygen mix to make water, or H_2O. These are not bad chemicals at all.

Our brains and bodies use special chemicals to communicate, which are called 'hormones'. There are various hormones, which give instructions to our brains and bodies and can make us feel different ways. It can help us to know where emotions come from because if we understand something, we are usually less afraid of it. It can be scary when we have big, strong feelings and we don't know why.

BUTTERFLIES IN OUR TUMMIES?

These aren't real. I'm just a bit **anxious.**

That brings us to the imaginary butterflies in our tummies! As you can see, Min knows they're not real too!

If our brains are afraid or worried about something, two hormones called adrenalin and cortisol are sent out around our bodies, in our blood. It's tricky to understand (unless you're a scientist, which you might be!) but those two hormones tell our bodies, 'Hey, you're in danger, you'd better get ready!' If our bodies are getting ready to protect ourselves, that's more important than digesting our lunch. So, our tummies don't need much blood supplying oxygen and other goodies, until our brains think we are safe again. We need blood in our arms and legs so we can run away if we need to. The tickly, squirmy feeling in our tummies comes because blood has moved to where we need it most.

Other things might happen too, like your heart beating faster or you needing to do a wee or a poo! That's our bodies making sure we are ready to protect ourselves without having to worry about going to the toilet. You might get a bit sweaty as well, especially on your hands. Lights might seem brighter. That is because our pupils dilate to let in more light to help us see, like a cat at night. Noises might seem louder, because our ears and brains are carefully listening for any dangers.

These things can happen to our bodies when we're stressed or afraid about something, or even when we are excited about something good.

So sometimes our emotions help to keep us safe. For example, if you were swimming at the beach and thought you saw a shark in the water, you might feel very afraid, and those hormones would help your legs and arms get you out of the water quickly. That's a good thing! But sometimes we might feel afraid of something that can't really hurt us, and it can be helpful to know what to do to feel better.

MIN AND PREPARING FOR CHANGES

Min is afraid of going to class and their teacher being away, and the class having a supply teacher who Min does not know, and who does not know Min. So, Min's parents get a message from Min's school if their teacher is going to be away, and Min knows to go to a different class for the day. Even though they are in a class with different meerkats, it is more important to Min that they know their teacher.

There are happy hormones too, like serotonin or endorphins. You know that kind of light, happy feeling you have when you have laughed a lot about something, or done some tough exercise? That's from endorphins. Our bodies also release endorphins if we are hurt, to help us feel better. Cool huh? Serotonin can help us feel calm, like the feeling we get if we are doing our favourite thing, and no one will disturb us.

HORMONES AND SENSATIONS

Do you feel anything in your body when something exciting is going to happen? What about when you are afraid about something? Maybe you'd like to find out about some of the other hormones that can cause sensations in our bodies?

⇌ Chapter 3 ⇋

How Can I Tell What Emotion I Am Feeling?

HOW CAN I TELL WHEN I AM FEELING SOMETHING?

It can be really tricky to work out what emotion you are feeling. Autistic people – like you and authors Yenn and Tanya – can find it really hard to work out what emotion they might be experiencing. Someone might tell you that you seem to be angry or sad or some other emotion, but it can be hard to know what that actually means.

The good thing is that there are ways to work out what emotion you are having. One of these is to listen to other people, so if someone you trust tells you that you seem angry, try to think about what is happening for you when they say this.

For example, are you throwing things, pacing up and down, wanting to punch something – or someone? Does your forehead feel tight? Do you feel hot? Or are there other things you do or sensations you feel when someone tells you that you are angry? This works just as well for other emotions as it does for anger.

Sometimes people use characters to describe their emotions. They might say anger is a red beast or jealousy is a green-eyed monster. Of course, these characters are not real things! Anger is an emotion, not a red beast that jumps on you when you are feeling angry! These characters are a way people talk about emotions which can help them to understand them better.

ACTIVITY: Emotions and characters

Do you ever turn the emotions you feel into characters? Can you think of any characters that you might call your emotions? Write your ideas below or on a piece of paper.

WHY DO I SOMETIMES FEEL AN EMOTION AND OTHER TIMES I DON'T?

Emotions can be tricky things. They don't always happen. One day something might make you feel sad or anxious and the next day the same thing won't make you feel anything. Some autistic people get anxious about their emotions and how they don't always make them feel the same. A good way of looking at this is to experience your emotions as they happen. You don't need to worry about emotions – they happen all the time – sometimes they are the same and sometimes they are different, and that is okay.

IS IT HARDER FOR AUTISTIC KIDS TO KNOW WHAT EMOTION THEY ARE FEELING?

In a word, yes! Some autistic people have something called 'alexithymia'. That is a big word which means that autistic people can struggle to be aware of what emotion they are feeling. It comes from some Ancient Greek words mixed together, like this: a (not) – lexis (words) – thymos (emotions). It is sometimes called emotion blindness too. It is a bit like how a blind person can't see the world around them with their eyes. Someone with emotion blindness can see the world around them but can't 'see' the emotions they are feeling. Alexithymia doesn't mean that we have no emotions – far from it! Autistic people have all the same sorts of emotions that everyone else does but it can be hard to feel them or be aware when they are happening. Emotion blindness often means that people feel nothing and then all of a sudden, they feel emotions very strongly.

MIN AND EMOTION BLINDNESS

Min has a really close friend called Ping. Min and Ping have loads of fun together, playing games and chatting. One day Ping tells Min that he has to go and live a long way away. Min will not see Ping face-to-face for a long time. Min knows in their mind that they should feel sad, and they are sad in their thoughts, but they can't feel sad in their emotions. Min worries that they are being horrible by not feeling sad about Ping leaving. In fact, Min is sad – they just can't feel it. Min isn't being horrible at all. It is perfectly okay to have emotion blindness. It doesn't mean you are being cold-hearted or mean, and you can't help having it.

EXPLORING YOUR EMOTIONS – SPOTTING WHAT EMOTIONS MAY FEEL LIKE AND WHAT THEY MIGHT MAKE YOU DO

Here is a list of things which might happen when you are feeling an emotion. There is some information on how you might feel in your mind and body and what you might do when you are having an emotion. You might have some things happen which are different to what is in this list – or you may not. Emotions are a very personal thing – we all have our own ways of experiencing them. This is perfectly okay.

Anxiety

What you might feel like and do when you are anxious:

- Feel as if your heart is racing.

- Feel tight in your chest.

- Need to go to the toilet.

- Have a tight feeling across your forehead.

- Have 'butterflies in your stomach'.

- Pace up and down.

- Stim and use a fidget.

- Worry about things – think about the same thing over and over.

- Have a shaking body.

- Have sweaty hands.

- Feel dizzy.

- Have dry mouth.

- Find it hard to swallow.

- Be unable to sleep at night.

Anger

What you might feel like and do when you are angry:

- Feel as if your heart is racing.

- Feel tightness in your chest.

- Yell.

■ Throw things.

■ Swear or say nasty words.

■ Want to run away.

■ Want to smash or hit things – or people.

■ Feel hot.

■ Have tears coming out of your eyes.

■ Clench your teeth or hands.

■ Feel as if you have lots of energy inside, as if you will explode (don't worry; you won't actually explode! ☺).

Happiness

What you might feel like and do when you are happy:

■ Feel good or light in your body.

■ Smile.

■ Laugh.

- Skip, dance or jump up and down.

- Stim/flap.

- Run.

- Clap.

- Want to be around other people, if that's what you like.

Excitement

What you might feel like and do when you are excited:

- Have 'butterflies' in your tummy.

- Need to move around a lot.

- Stim/flap.

- Run/dance/skip.

- Sing.

- Talk loudly.

- Tell everyone you meet about the thing that makes you excited.

- Be unable to sleep at night.

Sadness

What you might feel like and do when you are sad:

- Feel a 'sinking' or heavy feeling in your body, as if your arms and legs weigh much more than usual.

- Feel a tightness in your forehead.

- Feel 'hollow'.

- Want to spend time alone.

- Cry.

- Find it hard to swallow.

- Not want to do anything, even things you usually like.

Disgust

What you might feel like and do when you are disgusted:

- Feel sick, dry retch or be sick.

- Avoid the thing which is disgusting you.

- Run away.

Amusement

What you might feel like and do when you are amused:

- Have a giggly feeling in your tummy.

- Smile.

- Feel good or 'light' in your body.

- Laugh.

- Want the amusing thing to go on forever.

- Want to share the amusing thing with other people.

Fear

What you might feel like and do when you are afraid:

- Heart beats faster.

- Want to run away.

- Want to hide.

- Feel tightness in your chest.

- Scream.

- Cry.

- Breathe faster.

Surprise

What you might feel like and do when you are surprised:

- Breathe in quickly.

- Step backwards.

- Hold up your hands.

- Want to hide.

- Feel frightened.

- Feel excited.

MIXED EMOTIONS

Another thing to know about emotions is that we can have more than one at the same time! Sometimes they might even be opposites! That might sound a bit odd – and a bit worrying – but it does happen. Min the Meerkat has a story about this.

MIN AND MIXED EMOTIONS

Min is told that they have to go to a new class in school. In the new class, Min will get to build things – which is something they absolutely love. They are very excited about this and want to start right away. But Min is also anxious about the class because they don't know the other students who will be in the class, and they are afraid that the other kids might be mean. Min is feeling what is sometimes called 'mixed emotions', which is where you have more than one feeling going on at the same time.

Also, sometimes, if we have been really happy and done something fun, we might feel really sad just because it's over, and the contrast or change can make the sadness feel worse. Just give it some time, use your strategies (more on this later in the book) and you will get back into your comfort zone.

ACTIVITY: Your emotions

Do you have some emotions that you often feel? If so, do you know what they might be? Write them below or on a piece of paper.

. . . .

. . . .

. . . .

We hope this chapter on how to know what emotion you are feeling has helped you understand your emotions better.

⇌ Chapter 4 ⇋

What if I Don't Feel Anything in My Body?

ABOUT FEELING NOTHING

As we talked about earlier in this book, lots of autistic people find it really hard to feel their emotions. It doesn't mean we don't have emotions, but it can make life difficult. Some autistic people know when they are feeling emotions and what those emotions are, but many of us do not.

WHAT ARE SOME WORDS TO DESCRIBE HOW I AM FEELING?

There are lots of words we can use to describe emotions. Here are a few of them that you might know and maybe some new ones.

- terrified
- anxious
- scared
- happy
- excited
- disgusted
- even-tempered
- angry
- furious
- horrified
- despairing
- sad
- devastated
- bored

- curious
- confused
- delighted
- depressed
- joyful
- content
- tense
- relaxed
- ecstatic
- worried
- confident
- embarrassed
- shocked.

One thing you might have noticed is that what you might feel in your body can be the same for completely different emotions. This often happens when people feel anxiety or excitement. You can think of excitement as the nice version of anxiety – or alternatively anxiety as the less nice version of excitement! Your awareness of emotions is related to the hormones that your brain sends out to tell your body what it needs to do. Sometimes the same hormones are sent out in response to different emotions.

ACTIVITY: Naming your feelings

Have you felt like any of these words before? If so, which ones? Write them below or on a piece of paper.

. . . .

. . . .

. . . .

Have you felt like any words which aren't on this list? Write them below or on a piece of paper.

. . . .

. . . .

. . . .

CAN I LEARN HOW TO FEEL MY EMOTIONS?

Yes! You can definitely learn how to feel your emotions. It can be hard for autistic people to know what their emotions are but it's not impossible.

You can learn to understand what the different

emotions are and how it feels in your mind and body when you have them. It might be tricky and take practice, but you are amazing and can do amazing things – including feeling your emotions!

MIN AND LEARNING TO FEEL EMOTIONS

Min really finds it hard to know what they are feeling. When something sad happens, Min will cry but they don't feel different. Their mum says, 'But can't you tell that you are sad? You're crying.' But Min does not know they are sad. Their mum says, 'You can figure out if you are sad. When you are crying it usually means you are sad.' So now Min knows if they are crying that they are probably sad.

ACTIVITY: Your feelings

Do you know what any of your emotions feel like? What helps you to know you are feeling an emotion? Write your ideas below or on a piece of paper.

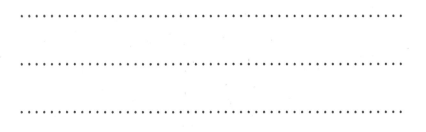

BUT ISN'T IT EASIER TO NOT FEEL ANYTHING?

Author Yenn has alexithymia – you might remember that the long word means you find it hard to feel emotions. Yenn only occasionally feels emotions, when they are very anxious or angry. They don't get angry much, but they are often anxious. For years, Yenn thought being unable to feel emotions was a good thing. They thought their emotions were primarily negative and feeling them was unpleasant. Yenn found out when they were an adult that there was a thing called alexithymia and realized this was something they experienced. After a while, Yenn realized that it probably wasn't all good because not feeling emotions until they were really big made life hard. Yenn is now better at working out what emotions they are feeling.

As Yenn discovered, there can be problems with not feeling emotions. Alexithymia often means that someone is experiencing emotions but is not aware of them. This is a really tricky thing. People can go from feeling nothing to instantly feeling a really strong emotion. This can be scary. It can mean they suddenly get very angry and yell or throw things, or that they are really sad. It is usually better to be able to know when you are feeling an emotion before it gets too strong and scary. Then you can use some strategies to help.

Chapter 5

What Things Might Scare My Brain?

DOES EVERYONE FEEL SCARED OR ANXIOUS SOMETIMES?

We all feel scared sometimes, even adults. And meerkats! There are some things that make most people feel scared, whether they're autistic or not. But there are some things that can make autistic people feel scared or anxious that don't usually scare non-autistic people, and these are often sensory scares.

We have talked about those chemicals in our bodies called hormones. The same hormones can make us feel scared or angry, anxious or worried. We all react differently to what's happening in our world. And some of the tips we talk about in this book can help you get back into your comfort zone, even if you're feeling scared, angry, anxious or worried. They can even work if you are so excited about something that it doesn't feel good in your body.

It's great that you can build a toolkit that works for **you**, no matter what big emotions you are feeling. Some things will work for some people and not others, so we need to try different things to know what will work for our own brains and bodies. We can call these things 'strategies'.

We can use our strategies when we have these feelings, or when we think we might get those feelings, like if you need to do something that's difficult and know that you might feel scared or anxious. An example might be if your parent has to have an operation in hospital to make them feel better. That can be a bit scary, even though you know that the doctors are going to help. You can start using your strategies before they go into hospital to help you feel a bit better.

Yenn feels scared when they see a spider or when they are out in the dark. Yenn has some strategies to help them manage when their emotions are difficult, like listening to music, writing, or talking to a friend. Tanya feels scared if she is going somewhere new and she doesn't know where she can park her car so she might be late. Being late makes her feel horrible and sometimes she can have a meltdown. But she has some strategies to help avoid that, like looking at online maps of where she can park her car and working out how long it will take to walk from the car to the place she is going. She always makes sure she is early and makes plans about what to do if she can't find a car park.

Min feels anxious or scared if they are going to be around a lot of other animals because they don't like it when other animals touch them unexpectedly. Mostly they avoid it but sometimes it happens unexpectedly.

SENSORY SCARES

Autistic people often have super senses and can detect things that non-autistic people can't. Have you ever smelled something really bad and said, 'Wow, that stinks!' and someone else said, 'I can't smell anything'? We all sense things differently, and whatever you sense is right for you. If anyone ever tells you that you're being silly for being upset about a bad smell or something, that is not okay. Maybe you could give them this book to read! There is a good side to having a strong sense of smell too – smelling something lovely can make our whole body feel happy and light. Tanya feels happy and light if she smells a lemon, grapefruit or orange, so smelling one of those can really help if she needs a mood boost.

You've probably heard about five senses at school or somewhere else – sight from our eyes, hearing from our ears, touch from our skin, smell from our noses, and taste from our tongues. But we have some senses about other things too, which you might not have heard about. They all have quite big and interesting names! We have:

- Vestibular – that is about balancing, so we know if we are upside down, or have leaned too far over and might fall. That sense is actually from inside our ears! So, we use our ears for two things. The word 'vestibular' comes from a Latin word, 'vestibulum', which means entrance. Isn't 'vestibulum' a great-sounding word?! Part of our ear canal is called a 'vestibule', maybe because that bit for balancing is at the entrance to our inner ears, safe inside our heads. Ears are complicated little things!

- Proprioception – that is about our body position and pressure inside our bodies. Sometimes it can feel good. Do you ever like to roll yourself tightly in a blanket, like a sausage roll? Or to put cushions on yourself and have a friend sit on you? Or wear some tight clothes? 'Proprioception' is a mash-up of two Latin words – 'proprius' (individual or own) and 'capio' (receive). So it means to receive signals or sense where our own body parts are in relation to each other, and where they are in the space around us. For example, if you close your eyes and put your arm up above your head, you might be able to feel that your arm is up high, even if you can't see it. You might even be able to touch your hands together under the bedclothes when you can't see them. Pretty amazing, huh?

- Interoception – that is about telling our brains what is going on inside our body, like feeling hungry or thirsty, or if we need to go to the toilet, or about our emotions. It can be very hard to know those things sometimes, especially if we are doing something really interesting and our brain is busy thinking about that. 'Interoception' comes from 'inter' which can mean among or inside, like 'interior'. Inter is mixed with 'capio', that we already know about. So interoception is about sensing things inside our bodies.

- Nociception – this is the sense that tells us if something in our body might be injured. It comes from another Latin word, 'nocere', which means to harm. Plus 'capio' again. So we are sensing that something in our body might be harmed and need fixing. We might feel that as pain. For example, if you stub your toe and it hurts, it's a good idea to check that your toenail is okay.

We don't normally get scared from those last four senses with big names, but our brains can get a fright from things we hear, see, smell, touch or taste.

ACTIVITY: Sensory scares

Can you think of any sensory scares you might have? This might be a specific noise or red lights on a machine, or a yucky smell, or something that gives you a fright when you accidentally touch it. Write your ideas below or on a piece of paper.

. . . .

. . . .

. . . .

SCARES FROM OUTSIDE OUR BODIES

There are some things that most people are scared of because they can be dangerous – it makes sense to be scared! That way our bodies can get ready to protect ourselves if we need to. An example might be if you woke up and found a crocodile on your bed. That would never happen of course but, if it did, it would be very sensible to feel scared.

Sometimes, we can feel scared if we are in a situation that has gone wrong before. For example, if you were riding a scooter one day and fell off when you went around a corner, your brain might feel scared the next few times you go around that corner because you had been hurt there before. After you've been safely around that corner enough times, your brain might not feel scared any more. Or maybe you just decide to go a different way!

Some people like feeling scared – you might have heard people say, 'What a rush!' They like the feeling they get from those hormones. You might like that too! That feeling is why some people like watching horror movies, or playing games that have scary moments in them, or riding a rollercoaster at a theme park. Other people don't like that feeling at all and so they don't do those things, or they might only like that feeling sometimes.

Do you think it's weird that we might feel scared if we saw a snake in the back garden, but we wouldn't feel scared if we saw the same one in a glass case at a zoo? It's cool that our brains sometimes know when we might be in danger and when we're not, when it's the same snake. And some people love snakes and aren't scared of them at all. How about you?

ACTIVITY: Sometimes scary

Can you think of any other things that might be scary sometimes and not scary other times, like the snake? Write them below or on a piece of paper.

. . . .

. . . .

. . . .

Why do you think they are only scary sometimes? Write your ideas below or on a piece of paper.

. . . .

. . . .

. . . .

Sometimes people can make us feel scared too, from something they say or do, or even just by being around them. If any people make you feel scared, it's best to tell an adult you trust about it and do your best to stay away from that person.

OTHER SCARES FROM INSIDE OUR BODIES

Sometimes our thoughts can make us feel scared, especially if we have a good imagination. Using our imagination can be wonderful, if we are doing some art or building something or writing a story. But not if we are imagining scary things. These scares are often the hardest to deal with, since we can't exactly get away from our own brain, in the same way we can get away from a bright buzzing light.

Sometimes adults will tell us that we're being silly and whatever we are scared of isn't real. Often, we know that, but it doesn't help that we know it's not real, because we still think about it and feel scared. We need to find some strategies to help us not think about those things, or not think about them as deeply or as often. We will talk more about that in the next chapter.

~ Chapter 6 ~

What Can I Do if My Brain Is Scared (Anxious, Overloaded)?

WHAT IS ANXIETY?

Anxiety is an emotion that happens when we are worried or concerned about something. Everyone experiences anxiety sometimes but for autistic folks it can be a big issue and we can feel anxious most or all of the time. Most people don't like to feel anxious. Being scared or afraid is like an intense version of anxiety. Sometimes we might feel anxious and not know why, but we usually know what we are scared about. Things that help if you feel anxious will help for feeling scared as well.

WHY DO WE GET ANXIOUS?

Like all emotions, anxiety happens for a reason.
Many, many years ago when human beings were a
new thing, anxiety was incredibly useful. Anxiety
and fear told our ancestors that they needed
to spring into action if something was going to
attack them. Those same hormones we talked
about (cortisol and adrenalin) would rush through
their brain and body telling them they were in
danger and had to do something to avoid getting
eaten by a sabre-tooth tiger (or some other
threat). Those hormones get our bodies ready to
face danger. There are five main things we do
when our brains feel under threat:

- Fight – meaning we should fight the threat.

- Flight – meaning we should run away.

- Freeze – meaning we should stay very still
  and hope the threat goes away.

- Fawn – meaning we should try and make
  friends with the threat.

- Flop – this is a bit like freezing, but our
  muscles go loose and floppy.

Imagine a big dog is chasing you and you get very scared and anxious. You could choose to fight the dog, flee (run away) from the dog, freeze (stay very still and hope it goes away), fawn (hold out your hand to the dog and say, 'good doggie' and hope it doesn't attack you) or flop (go loose and floppy and hope it doesn't hurt as much if the dog jumps on you).

The problem is that these days there aren't a lot of things we face which could actually threaten our physical health. We don't walk down the street and see a sabre-tooth tiger on the footpath. The stress, fear or anxiety hormones for humans these days are the same as if there were physical threats. But the threats we actually have are quite different from those our prehistoric ancestors faced. This can make our anxiety very difficult to deal with. There is also the issue of time. Our ancestors experienced threats which tended to be quite quick. The anxiety hormones would do their job and then go away. But for people with anxiety in the modern world, the 'threats' can go on for a long time.

ACTIVITY: Your threat response

What do you think you would do if you were under threat? Would you fight, flee, freeze, fawn or flop – or something else? Write your thoughts below or on a piece of paper.

. . . .

. . . .

. . . .

WHAT CAN MAKE ME FEEL ANXIOUS?

There are a lot of things which make us anxious. For Yenn, their anxiety has changed over their lifetime. They used to be worried about employment, then they were worried about home maintenance and lately they have been worried about being hacked online. Yenn has never worried about some of the things other people worried about. They have never worried about an exam or their school work – when they were at school – but for many people these things are very stressful.

Tanya worries about people asking her questions about herself, about not being able to find a car park if she is going somewhere new, and about accidentally hurting other people's feelings and then they won't like her any more.

We all have different things that make us stressed, anxious or afraid. Autistic people often experience anxiety. It is nothing to feel ashamed about, but it can feel horrible so it's a good idea to find strategies to help.

WHAT CAN I DO TO FEEL LESS ANXIOUS?

There are a lot of things that people do to feel less anxious. Some people practise meditation, some do deep breathing, some listen to music, do exercise, or something else. If you find something which makes you feel less anxious that is really helpful. You might find pleasant sensory experiences can help. Yenn uses a weighted lap band with blue and purple sequins on it, so they get nice physical and visual relief from anxiety and overwhelm at the same time. Tanya likes to knit something very complicated, so she has to focus hard on that, and it helps her stop thinking about what is making her anxious. Plus, she chooses very soft yarns that feel nice to knit with.

If you can, it is helpful to find out information about the thing that is making you feel anxious.

For example, if you are going somewhere new, you can look at pictures of it on the internet and make a plan about what to do when you are there. Often, we worry about things that we are uncertain about, so if we can be more certain or sure about it, we feel less anxious.

MIN GOING TO SCHOOL CAMP

Min has a school camp coming up. They really want to go, as it is at an ecology centre and they are very interested in the environment. But they are worried about the food – most meerkats eat lots of different foods, including insects, but Min is vegetarian and can't eat insects. They are also worried about who will be sleeping in their room. So, Min, their parents and their teacher work out a plan so that Min will share a room with their friends and can take their own food just in case they can't eat the other food at camp. Now Min isn't as anxious.

It can also help to just not do something if it is causing a lot of anxiety, especially if it's not essential. This is something you could talk to a parent or carer about. Sometimes something really stresses us out and we think we have to keep doing it anyway (such as going to the supermarket to do grocery shopping, if that makes you anxious) but this is not always the case. Often there will be a different way to do things that will mean you can avoid doing something that really stresses you out.

Here are some strategies to help manage your anxiety:

- Do a physical activity, such as jumping on a trampoline, running or dancing.

- Lie under a weighted blanket or weighted toy.

- Use a fidget.

- Stim.

- Listen to music.

- Find out more information so that you know more about the thing that is making you feel anxious.

- Play with pets/assistance animals.

- Do something outside in nature, maybe some gardening or picking up rubbish at the park.

- Talk about what is making you anxious with a parent or carer – or health professional, like a doctor.

- Watch a movie or TV show that you like.

- Do something you love – like an interest.

- Read a book.

- Play a video game.

- Write stories or poetry or do some art.

- Make a list.

- Take medication for anxiety, if you wish to.

- Don't do the thing that is causing anxiety (if possible).

MIN AND HELPING WITH ANXIETY

Min gets quite anxious about a number of different everyday things – meeting new people, their work at school and riding on the bus. When they are anxious, they listen to music on their headphones or they make something, or both! They also have a weighted toy cat that they put on their lap and pat. These things help Min to feel less anxious.

CAN ANXIETY FEEL LIKE SOMETHING ELSE?

Anxiety can show up in a number of ways. One of these is anger. Someone who is really anxious may find themselves getting angry and irritated and not realize it. So, if you feel angry, you might actually be anxious.

Anxiety is quite tiring. Basically, your body is on high alert for danger for a long time. You can imagine that this is challenging! If you can calm down from feeling anxious this is likely to give you more energy to do the things you like doing.

ARE THERE ANY GOOD THINGS ABOUT BEING ANXIOUS?

There are some positives to being anxious. Imagine if you never worried about anything? You might walk in front of cars on the street or pat a wild tiger! Anxiety is part of what stops us from doing unsafe things, so it definitely has a purpose. It is just that when it goes on for a long time and you feel there is nothing you can do about it, it becomes a problem.

⇒ Chapter 7 ⇐

What Will Help if My Brain Feels Angry?

Remember when we talked about what we might do or feel when we are angry? It doesn't usually feel good to be angry so it's helpful to find our way back to our comfort zone.

WHAT CAN I DO WHEN I THINK I MIGHT GET ANGRY?

If you know something is going to happen that might make you feel angry (let's call these 'tricky things'), it's a great idea to work out some strategies to help **before** the tricky thing happens. It might be something that involves lots of people being around, or something that you are afraid of doing, or something that's noisy, bright or smelly (or all three!). Or maybe you've been really excited about something and then it doesn't happen, so you are very disappointed. That's really hard, so it's good to have a plan just in case. Lots of things can make our brains feel angry and it can help a lot to work out what to do before it happens.

If something has happened that makes you feel anxious or angry, it's a good idea to talk about it with a parent or other trusted adult. You can work together on a plan or strategies to help for next time. For example, if someone is coming to visit your home and you know they have a loud voice and wear really strong perfume that gives you a headache and makes you feel angry, there are some strategies that might help:

- Your parent could meet the person somewhere else.

- Your parent could spend time with that person outside while you are inside (or the other way around) and not ask you to talk to that person.

- Your parent could ask that person to not wear that perfume when they come to visit and to talk more quietly. Sometimes parents don't like to do this because they think it's rude, but it really isn't. You have the right to be comfortable in your home.

- Your parent can keep the visit short.

- You could wear noise-cancelling headphones, use a fidget, and stay in another room doing something you like.

- You could visit a friend if you have one close by.

Can you think of anything else that might help? Min used some strategies to help and isn't feeling angry.

It's great to have a portable kit for when we need to do tricky things. You can use it for feeling angry, anxious, afraid or stressed. Not everything helps everybody (and sometimes nothing helps, especially if we didn't know the tricky thing was going to happen) but here are some ideas for what to keep in your kit:

- A water bottle and snack – crunchy snacks can be helpful, if you like them.

- Noise-cancelling headphones or ear defenders.

- A hat or cap or sunglasses to block out light.

- A blanket – it could be a heavy weighted one if that helps you, or a light one to put over yourself like a tent.

- Your favourite fidgets, like a spinner, some putty, or something else.

- A device to play a game on or listen to music. It can help to breathe deeply while listening to music.

- A book.

- Something to chew.

- Some art supplies.

- Something you like the smell of.

Tanya takes her knitting everywhere (it's like a fidget), plus her headphones. Yenn takes their phone and headphones with them wherever they go.

ACTIVITY: Tricky things kit

What would you put in your tricky things kit? You can use some of the ideas in this book, with some of your own ideas, or whatever you like. Write your ideas below or on a piece of paper.

. . . .

. . . .

. . . .

. . . .

. . . .

Maybe you already have a kit. Is there anything you would change about it? Write your ideas below or on a piece of paper.

. . . .

. . . .

MANAGING OUR TRICKY THINGS

It's also important not to have too many tricky things close together. We might be okay with one tricky thing, but if we have to do two close together, like going to school then going straight to the shops, that can make us feel angry or upset because our brains need a break.

When we are kids, sometimes we don't have a lot of choice about when we have to do tricky things, but it's something we can talk with our parent or carer about. Maybe they could have a look at this book with you because learning how to recognize, handle and use our anger is really hard and all people need help from others to do that.

WHAT CAN I DO IF I AM ALREADY ANGRY?

Sometimes if we are angry, our bodies feel as if they have **lots** of energy that has to come out. It's kind of like a volcano erupting. We might yell a lot, or we might kick or punch things, or we might throw things. We might not feel so good afterwards if our anger comes out like that because we might have hurt ourselves, or another person, or broken something that we really like.

Those are not very helpful strategies to use for anger, but it often takes **a long time** to be able to use some other ones. The best strategy is learning about what might make us angry (those tricky things) and finding ways to make them easier and to help us deal with them.

You will need some help from trusted adults, like a parent, or a teacher, or maybe you see someone else you can talk to about some other ways to get that energy out. We all need help to learn these strategies. There are some adults who still yell or throw things when they are angry too, and we understand that it's very hard to find and use other strategies. Our brains take a long time to learn how to handle big emotions like anger, and plenty of people never learn how. So, give yourself a free pass if it doesn't happen quickly ☺.

When we already feel angry, it's hard to think very clearly. Sometimes, if a person suggests something that could help us feel better, we feel even more angry! And if someone tells us to 'just calm down', that is the worst!

If you can get away from the tricky thing that's making you feel angry, that's great. Then it's just about using your strategies to get back to your comfort zone, without having to keep dealing with the tricky thing.

Here are some things that help to get that energy out:

- Yelling and jumping up and down really hard on a pillow (Tanya learned to use a pillow after jumping up and down really hard on concrete and hurting her leg).

- Smashing a cardboard box with a broom stick.

- Pulling weeds out of the garden as fast as you can.

- Having someone you trust breathe deeply with you.

- Running, jumping on a trampoline, doing star jumps or push-ups, dancing, or something else that uses a lot of energy and makes us feel a bit puffed.

ACTIVITY: Using up your angry energy

Can you think of any other ways to use up our angry energy? Are there any ways you use up your angry energy? You can write your ideas below or on a piece of paper. Or maybe you could make a poster with ideas. You can always add to it, or cross things off.

. . . .

. . . .

. . . .

HOW CAN MY ANGER BE HELPFUL?

Sometimes, autistic people have what we can call a strong sense of 'social justice'. This is when we care a lot about whether things are fair, how people and animals are treated, how we look after our environment, and other things that affect a lot of people.

When we care a lot about something, it can make us feel angry if others don't care about it.

We mentioned Greta Thunberg earlier in this book. Greta is autistic and cares **a lot** about the environment and climate change. Caring for our environment is important for everyone. Greta felt angry that world leaders did not seem to think it was a big emergency like they (and a lot of scientists) did. So, they decided to do their best to make people listen and then a lot more people started talking and thinking about climate change. Most people don't have the energy to do something as big as Greta did, but we can do smaller things to help the environment, like using fabric bags instead of plastic bags, or taking a 'naked lunch' to school, where your food is in containers you can use again, instead of wrapping that you throw in the bin. Doing small things like this with their family is how Greta started.

MIN USING THEIR ANGER TO HELP

Min feels angry about their local park having a lot of rubbish on the ground. That can cause problems for animals as well as the environment. Sometimes if we do something about what is making us feel angry, that can do two good things – help us not feel angry any more and help to fix the problem! Min has a cool grabber to pick up rubbish and put in a bag when they go to the park. They like to pretend it is a robot arm. Their friend, Ziggy, has one too. The added good thing is that being outside in the park can help our brains make more serotonin (that's the hormone that helps us feel calm).

ACTIVITY: Using your anger

Can you think of any big problems in the world that make you feel angry? Or maybe a small thing? Can you think of any small ways that you could help? Write your ideas below or on a piece of paper.

Chapter 8

What Can I Do to Help My Brain Stay Calm?

WHAT TAKES ME OUT OF MY COMFORT ZONE?

Lots of things can take us out of our emotional comfort zone – things like someone being mean to us, things not going the way we planned, something that upsets our senses like a nasty smell or loud noise. Every person has different things that make them feel uncomfortable or even really awful.

There are different ways of feeling bad – we might feel sad or stressed or disappointed or scared or angry.

MIN AND FEELING ANGRY

Min saves up their money and orders a cool new case for their tablet. They order it online, so it is coming in the post. It should only take two days to arrive, but Min is still waiting after two weeks! Whenever the postman comes and the case doesn't arrive, Min feels hot and wants to throw things. Sometimes they do, or they yell at their parents to get out of their room. Min is angry and that's normal – sometimes if something we expect doesn't happen and we really want it to, we might feel disappointed or sad. Or sometimes we might feel angry. It can be extra hard if it is something we can't fix, like when post is delayed, and we just have to wait.

Min's parents help Min to distract themselves with other things so Min doesn't think about it all day, but they still feel angry when the post comes. Eventually it arrives, and the tablet fits into it perfectly.

WHAT CAN HELP ME STAY IN MY COMFORT ZONE?

The good thing about feeling bad is that there are ways that we can make ourselves feel better, like we talked about in the chapters about how to help if you feel scared or angry. We talked about those separately because they are common **big** emotions that we feel. Strategies to help us feel calm and stay in our comfort zone are things we should do all the time.

We can do things that help us to feel calm and make our brains more comfortable. Some of this is about working out how to become calm before things get too much. Sometimes, if our emotions get overwhelming and build up, we have a meltdown. A meltdown is when we get stressed, and everything gets to be too much. We can hurt ourselves or break things or yell when we have a meltdown. Or sometimes we keep it all inside – some people call that a 'shutdown'. Either way feels horrible. Strategies to get back in our comfort zone will work a lot better if we do them before we get to the place where we feel overloaded and have a meltdown.

You can think of the emotions that make you feel bad as being like a pot of water on the cooker. The water gradually heats and heats without you noticing it and then, all of a sudden, it boils over. If a meltdown or shutdown is a bit like the pot boiling, it is best to do something to calm down before the 'pot' gets to boiling point.

You can learn how to make feelings calm down before they 'boil over' by doing things that you know help you to stay in your comfort zone. You might think this is impossible, and it does take time to learn, but it is absolutely possible to calm down if you are having difficult emotions. This is something you can work on, and you will probably need some help from your parents or other trusted adults. And you will get better the more you try. It is about finding things to do that help you feel calmer, so you can be in your comfort zone more.

ALL ABOUT 'STRATEGIES'

When we talk about feelings – and especially feeling bad – one thing that is often mentioned is strategies. What does this mean? You might think of a strategy as being something the army has or the decisions you make in a game. But there are also strategies that make emotions and feelings less difficult. A strategy is a thing you can do which can help to make your emotions go from horrible and scary to back in your comfort zone.

Everyone – including you – has different strategies to help them address tricky emotions and stay calm. You might not have thought about this before, but everyone has strategies, even if they don't know it! It can help to know what strategies you use so that you can know what might help when you are having a tough time, and maybe you can add to those strategies.

Knowing what other autistic people do to stay calm can help you as well. Here are some strategies that lots of autistic people – including the authors of this book – use to stay calm or become calm:

- Listening to music.

- Spending time alone.

- Using a fidget.

- Singing.

- Writing.

- Making art.

- Doing puzzles.

- Lying in a hammock or egg chair.

- Bouncing on a trampoline.

- Gaming.

- Rocking or dancing.

- Talking to a good friend or family member.

- Spending time on a passion ('special interest').

- Being with pets.

- Watching TV/movies.

- Being in an enclosed space.

- Being in nature.

- (Yenn says, 'writing, art and kitties – yay!!' And Tanya says, 'knitting and building Lego spaceships – yay!!')

MIN'S SUPER STRATEGIES

When Min is feeling stressed or anxious, they know that they need to be alone in a quiet place. Min has a wardrobe which is big enough for them to fit inside. It has a bean bag, cushions, coloured lights and pictures of Min's favourite things. Whenever Min is really stressed or sad, they get into their wardrobe and listen to music with their headphones on. This is Min's strategy for those feelings. When Min is already angry, their strategies include jumping up and down on the trampoline or running around the garden and yelling.

ACTIVITY: Staying in your comfort zone

Do you do anything to help you stay in your comfort zone? Do you have a special place to go at home? Do you have a favourite game or show? Do you like to use art or music? Or hit a fence with a pool noodle? Or do you have something else that helps you stay or become calm? Write your ideas below or on a piece of paper.

. . . .

. . . .

. . . .

. . . .

. . . .

. . . .

. . . .

DO I NEED DIFFERENT STRATEGIES FOR DIFFERENT FEELINGS?

Sometimes a different strategy is used for different feelings. For example, anger and sadness will probably need different strategies as they are emotions that make you feel quite different from one another – most of the time!

But different emotions can feel similar and when this happens it might be a good idea to use a similar strategy for these emotions. Feeling overloaded is often quite similar to feeling stressed so the strategy you use for one may help with the other. Knowing what helps when you are having one or other feeling is a good idea. It means that the next time you have trouble with one emotion you know what to do to help feel better. It can take a while to figure out what helps, though.

HOW CAN I TELL WHEN I AM IN MY COMFORT ZONE?

It can be difficult to know when we are calm and in our comfort zone, especially if we spend a lot of our time having emotions that make us feel bad. So, what does our comfort zone feel like? That is probably different for everyone – including you –

but there are a few things that can help you know you are feeling calm. When you are in your comfort zone you might find that you:

- feel good

- don't worry about anything

- think about nice things and look forward to fun activities

- don't have thoughts going around and around in your mind

- feel relaxed or even sleepy

- feel a light sensation in your body

- feel unusual, if most of the time you are having emotions that give you a hard time

- feel less stressed than you usually feel.

Being in your comfort zone is fantastic. It can be difficult, though, and even a lot of adults struggle with this so don't feel bad if you don't master it in one go – or 10 or 100 goes! One thing about getting into your emotional comfort zone is that it is something most people need to practise. **A lot**! The chances are it will not happen for you straight away! This is perfectly okay. It will happen at some point. It doesn't need to be unpleasant, though. In fact, working on feeling calmer can be a lot of fun and involve doing things you really enjoy, as that makes your brain happy.

And this is the end of the book. We hope it helps you to understand about your emotions and feelings and how to find your very own brilliant 'comfort zone'. Being autistic can be awesome and autistic kids have a lot of great things to share with the world. If you can understand your feelings and emotions, it can make your life much easier and help you to feel good and do good things. Remember that you are an amazing, super, awesome autistic kid! Keep being wonderful!

ONE FINAL ACTIVITY...

What are three things you know about your feelings and emotions after reading this book? Write them below or on a piece of paper.

. . . .

. . . .

. . . .

What are some ways you can find your comfort zone? Write them below or on a piece of paper.

· ·

· ·

· ·

· ·

Hoping you find your comfort zone,

Tanya and Yenn